The
Xenophobe's
guide to
KIWIS

Christine Cole Catley
Simon Nicholson

Oval Books

Published by Oval Books
335 Kennington Road
London SE11 4QE
United Kingdom

Telephone: +44 (0)20 7582 7123
Fax: +44 (0)20 7582 1022
E-mail: info@ovalbooks.com
Web site: www.ovalbooks.com

First published by Ravette Publishing, 1996
Reprinted 1997

First published by Oval Books, 2001
Updated 2003
New Edition 2005, updated 2006

Editor – Catriona Tulloch Scott
Series Editor – Anne Tauté

Cover design – Jim Wire
Printer – Liberdúplex Spain
Producer – Oval Projects Ltd.

Xenophobe's® is a Registered Trademark.

Cover: for the use of the Māori canoe bailer and
decorative headband, thanks are given to
Kiwifruits, The New Zealand Shop,
6 Royal Opera Arcade, London SW1

ISBN-13: 978-1-903096-87-1
ISBN-10: 1-903096-87-1

Contents

The Kiwi population is 4 million, compared with 19 million Aussies, 50 million English, 126 million Japanese, 238 million Indonesians and 300 million Americans.

New Zealand is more than twice the size of England and as big as Italy – without the toe, but could fit into Australia 28 times.

Nationalism and Identity

Forewarned

God's own country – 'Godzone' – is how Kiwis see New Zealand. They live in a land of unsurpassed natural beauty, friendly welcomes, fair play for one and all, and happily ever afters.

Give Kiwis half a chance and they will go out of their way to prove it to you. Indeed, visitors to New Zealand can expect to be constantly set upon by the insatiably hospitable locals. A quick chat with a passing Kiwi on any New Zealand street can very quickly turn into an invitation to dinner, a weekend stay in the spare room, or an extended guided tour of the local sights. Kiwis are fiercely proud of their country and love nothing better than to show it off.

So heaven help the visitors who criticise Godzone, especially if they come from the original European seedbeds – England, Scotland, Wales, or Ireland – and therefore should know better. Only the Aussie visitor is given leeway to criticise. Kiwi-bashing is, for some reason that escapes the Kiwis, a favourite Aussie pastime. In fact, you're about as likely to come across an Aussie with good feeling for the Kiwis as of finding a decent Australian beer.

Kiwis love receiving praise about their country. However, since self-deprecation is wired deeply into the national psyche, praise is always looked upon suspiciously. Kiwis constantly fear that they are being buttered up, or somebody is having them on. In keeping with this schizophrenic aspect of the national character, both praise and criticism are reported by the media, and are hotly debated. When English critic and columnist Bernard Levin devoted two columns in *The Times* to the incomparable beauties of New Zealand, this could not go unchallenged. During prime-time news on New Zealand's most popular television channel a reporter telephoned Levin and quoted to him his own words: "The loveliest country in the world?" Levin: "Yes, yes." "But do

1

you really mean it?" Levin: "Of course." "Yes, but really …?"

Travellers must therefore tread a delicate course, at first ladling out praise about New Zealand to allow the beaming local to demur, but then being willing to smile indulgently as he or she swiftly counters with a list of the country's faults. New Zealand may be Godzone, but no self-respecting Kiwi would wish to get too carried away in talking it up.

How Others See Them

'Friendly' is the adjective which crops up most in surveys about how others see the Kiwis. Except in the surveys taken by the Aussies, that is. The Aussies see the Kiwis as a bit stodgy and generally behind the times. Kiwis understand that these jibes are simply a product of envy, or sunstroke.

Perhaps a little ironically for a people who take their nickname from a timid, flightless bird, Kiwis are ardent travellers. There are more passports in New Zealand for each million people than in any other country in the world, and they get plenty of use. Kiwis can be found propping up bars and setting up camp in rugby stadiums around the globe. Overseas, Kiwis are usually sought after, whether as team leaders, nannies or for any other job requiring stamina, resilience, and versatility. Kiwis have to be versatile. There really aren't enough of them for there to be specialists.

How They Would Like to be Seen

The Kiwis know they take rather more interest in other countries than other countries take in them. This grieves them a little though they say politely that it's a natural consequence of being few in number, and living at the bottom of the map.

In fact, Kiwis enjoy nothing more than a chance to educate those who live under a cloud of ignorance concerning their country. A common preoccupation of Kiwis abroad is watching out for their nation's name in their host country's newspapers. Twice in three months is considered good going, even if the first mention concerns a natural disaster and the second is confined to the sports pages.

Still, Kiwis are quick to remind others about their country's successes. Conversations with Kiwis are often studded with references to the deeds of their famous fellows. There are four nationals few would question as being well-known abroad: mountaineer Edmund Hillary, writer Katherine Mansfield, nuclear scientist Ernest Rutherford, and opera singer Kiri Te Kanawa.

This is thought to be an absurdly short list in view of New Zealand's overall contribution to the world. So expect other prominent figures to be casually dropped to into conversations, including Godfrey Bowen, once the world's fastest sheep shearer, William Atack, the first man to use a whistle to stop a sports fixture, and Ernest Godward, inventor of the spiral hairpin. For just about any category of event or exploit, Kiwis will be able to come up with the name of a countryman or woman who deserves mention.

The Kiwis would like to be seen as people of consequence living in a country with much to offer the rest of the world. They want everyone to know that New Zealand is not just a source of naturally springy wool (used, by the way, to make championship tennis balls and award winning fashion by famous designers like Karen Walker, who's a Kiwi, in case you didn't know). As a first step they wish the rest of the world would learn just where they are on the globe, and colour it clean green.

Kiwis would prefer to believe that the world's ignorance of many matters about New Zealand is merely due to the fact that other countries have not achieved their degree of cultivation. It's a belief often reinforced by visitors who touch down at Auckland airport thinking that the next leg of their tour will be a bus ride to Sydney.

Special Relationships

For years the Kiwis suffered from reverse paranoia, the conviction that everyone who counted was out to be nice to them. This did not surprise them. They knew that deep down they were good keen men and women, lovable even.

Their strongest bond was with Britain, the Mother Country, the Old Country, Home – always expressed with capital letters. Kiwis were more thoroughly British than the British. What other country set up a Coronation Rejoicing Committee? In trade, in attitudes, in peace and in war, they were as one. Then Britain entered the European Community and ceased giving priority to New Zealand's principal exports of butter, meat and wool. Worse, Kiwis travelling to the Mother Country had to join the Heathrow queues marked 'Aliens'. It was a hard blow for an infant nation.

Despite such tribulations, by and large Kiwis still love Britain best. But signs of republicanism are breaking through. It isn't easy, coping with unrequited love.

The Kiwis also have a special relationship with the Americans. This began in the Second World War when New Zealand was used as a training and staging post for thousands of marines bound for the war in the Pacific and host families developed close ties with 'their' marine.

Because of this closeness with Americans, Kiwis were shocked by the way the U.S. government reacted to the Kiwi nuclear-free policy of the 1980s which prevented access of American nuclear-powered naval vessels to New Zealand's territorial waters. The U.S. took it as an insult and a snub and cast New Zealand out of the three-power

ANZUS defence alliance. This caused the Kiwi government some anxiety, given that the entirety of their domestic armed forces would fit comfortably into the galley of an American aircraft carrier. Nonetheless, the country steadfastly held its ground, and New Zealand continues with its nuclear-free stance.

During the tensest days of the nuclear disagreement Kiwis took heart from the fact that not all Americans sided with their government. A popular bumper sticker in the U.S., frequently photographed and sent to friends in New Zealand, read, 'Wish I Were a Kiwi Nuclear-Free'. Relationships have gradually improved and Americans visit in large numbers. Kiwis like them, and not just because of their amusing T-shirts and fat wallets.

The anti-nuclear stand was enormously strengthened when the French resumed their nuclear testing at Mururoa Atoll. Incensed that this should be happening in their Pacific backyard, Kiwis, backed by the Aussies, led the united South Pacific opposition, demanding that the French conduct their underground nuclear tests a little closer to home (preferably under the Arc de Triomphe). Kiwis are not an especially zealous people, but the Americans and French between them brought about an almost religious conversion of the entire country to the anti-nuclear banner.

Ultimately, though, it is Australians with whom Kiwis have the closest relationship. Each provides the other's largest number of visitors and there is a great deal of trade and intermarriage and crossings of 'the ditch' (Tasman Sea) in both directions for study and work. Periodic suggestions that New Zealand become the 'eighth state of Australia' are fodder for cartoonists and derisive pub talk. The Kiwis like to think that they can take on the Aussies at almost anything, and if you can lick them, why join them?

Whenever the Aussies show a distressing tendency to beat them at sport, Kiwis consider it a blip in the system, an aberration in the natural order of things. New Zealand horses always win the Melbourne Cup. If they don't, they should. New Zealand yachts beat the Aussies' yachts. The All Blacks expect to beat the Aussies at rugby. Kiwis know that when the Aussies win it's only because they have five times as many people to draw upon, or that, given their rather dubious national pedigree, they're only too happy to resort to underhand tactics.

The Kiwis do not need the Aussies' sheep jokes reminding them that New Zealand has far more sheep than it has people. There are close to 40 million of them, and they graze almost everywhere. Australia, they point out, actually has far more sheep. Aussie sheep, though, have the good sense to stay well away from cities so they don't have to cope with unwanted attention from the locals.

How They See One Another

Kiwis see themselves as one people with two main cultural groups: Māori and European. The latter are called *Pakeha* in the Māori language. The term is in common usage (many non-Māori Kiwis refer to themselves as *Pakeha*), but its origins and original meaning are a bit murky. The most likely derivation is from the old Māori word *Pakepakeha*, the term used by the Māori to describe a breed of mythical, mischievous, fair-skinned creatures. Considering the shock that Captain Cook and his original band of explorers must have generated with their first visit to New Zealand, it is hardly surprising that Europeans were at first thought to be supernatural imps.

As most *Pakeha* are descended from United Kingdom stock, telephone directories contain predominantly old English names together with pages of O', Mc, and Mac. A good 15% of the population identifies itself as Māori, but the directories do not give much indication of this

6

fact. This is because intermarriage has given at least half of them old English names and names beginning with O', Mc and Mac.

More recently, large numbers of Pacific Islanders have settled in New Zealand. The migration has been extensive. There are now more Niueans and Cook Islanders in Auckland than there are in Niue or the Cooks, and the same will soon be true of other islands. One can thus get a Pacific Islands experience without actually having to go there.

An influx of Asians, Eastern Europeans and all manner of exotic immigrants has given a much more cosmopolitan flavour to Kiwi society in recent years, and means that the country's 'bi-cultural' tag is now increasingly imprecise. At the weekends, city parks come alive with groups practising Tai Chi, throwing rugby balls, or playing games of Polynesian . No one group has yet worked out a way to combine all of these activities, though given the Kiwi entrepreneurial spirit, there is bound to be someone who is trying.

Of its population of 4 million, nearly three-quarters live in five main centres. One of these considers itself to be the only one that counts. In fact, it could be said that there are two geographic and psychic identities in New Zealand – Aucklanders, and The Rest.

Kiwis all accept that Auckland is the biggest city. After that, opinions vary depending on where one lives: Aucklanders are either self-centred, brash and quick to pick up foolish overseas fads; or they are exciting, innovative, outward-looking, and living in the country's leading city, the one with the best climate. The image Auckland projects to the rest of the country is aided (or not) by its 328 metre-high Sky Tower. Kiwis in the rest of the country suspect that the soaring, distinctively shaped monument is meant to make up for feelings of inadequacy. But Aucklanders are inordinately proud of the structure, happily reporting to one and all that it's the tallest building in the Southern Hemisphere*.

Not all of Auckland's record-breaking achievements, however, are worth bragging about. The city has the dubious honour of having suffered the 'longest blackout in peacetime'. In 1998, all four of the main cables that supplied power to downtown Auckland failed at the same time, leaving much of the city in the dark for 66 days. If it wasn't for the fact that around this time Sydney's residents were having to boil their water to ensure its safety, Kiwis everywhere would never have heard the end of it.

Character

The Kiwis are still so close to the official beginning of their country in 1840 (the year that 'The Treaty of Waitangi' was signed between Māori chiefs and the British Crown) that their character still reflects the dangers, privations and challenges of pioneering. They remain doers rather than dreamers, even if most of the doing these days is done within the confines of the suburban quarter-acre.

Pioneering Spirit

The Kiwis know theirs is the world's most spectacular scenery and, with its lakes, waterfalls, hot springs, active volcanoes, primeval forests and wild, wind-swept coasts, the most truly memorable. Situated where the Pacific plate meets the Tasman plate, New Zealand is visited by more vulcanologists and geologists than anywhere else in the

* Kiwis enjoy letting the words 'Southern Hemisphere' roll off their lips. If something is the biggest, fastest or best 'in the Southern Hemisphere', it sounds much more important than just 'the biggest in New Zealand'.

world. It also has magnificent mountains. Because of the mountains, bands of cloud form, especially over the Southern Alps, that look from a distance like a straight line in the pure blue sky which is why the Māori name for New Zealand is *Aotearoa*, 'the land of the long white cloud'.

The first Kiwis – the Māori – arrived in New Zealand from their mythical homeland Hawaiki around 800–1,000 years ago. Different groups, arriving on different *waka* (canoes), established coastal settlements around much of the country. The resource-rich landmass of New Zealand proved something of a paradise for the new arrivals. With basic needs relatively simple to take care of, the various *iwi* (tribes) had plenty of time for the more interesting enterprises of inter-tribal warfare and the invention of tongue-twisting place names*.

Europeans began to arrive in New Zealand from the late 1700s, originally pursuing seals, whales, and trade. Settlers and farmers soon followed.

Most of New Zealand was covered with dense bush so pioneers had to be rugged and self-reliant to make a go of it in their new land. Independence and ingenuity remain defining features of the Kiwi identity. A pioneering Kiwi 'joker' (also known as a bloke, chap or mate) soon learned that pioneers didn't make a fuss. Grin and bear it was the motto (but grumble all you like). They became dab hands at cutting down and burning trees, hurtling up and down mountains, and leapfrogging rivers. They had to, to get anywhere. This pioneering spirit became known

* Among an array of place names that baffle outsiders, the Kiwis can claim one of the world's longest. A hill in the Hawkes Bay is called Taumata-whaka-tangi-hanakoauau-o-Tamatea-turipukaka-pikimaunga-horo-nuku-pokai-whenuakutana-tahu. The name roughly means: the summit of the hill, where Tamatea, who is known as the land eater, slid down, climbed up and swallowed mountains, played on his nose flute to his loved one.

9

as Giving It a Go, whether or not you felt capable or had done it before.

Hostess to party newcomer: Can you play the piano?
Guest: No, but I'll give it a go.

The pioneering spirit and challenges go together. In 1986 in Paris, a Kiwi named A.J. Hackett having nothing better to do decided to attach a rope to his ankles and throw himself from the Eiffel Tower. He called this mind-boggling experience 'bungy' jumping. His company can now claim to have sent thousands of innocents plunging earthwards from bridges and cantilevered platforms all over the globe, the only thing between them and the next world being a stout rubber cord (made of the same stuff as condoms) secured to their ankles.

Against all the evidence, contemporary Kiwis persist in thinking of themselves as 'outdoorsy'. Man Against the Elements is a favourite entertainment theme, especially if it is something that can be watched on television in the comfort of your own home.

The Fair Go Concept

Kiwis are passionate about equality. Any perceived injustice or ill-treatment is met with united cries of "Fair go, mate". This egalitarian streak and sense of teamwork bucks the class system left behind in the Mother Country. Giving someone a fair go means offering every opportunity for them to rise to (but not necessarily above) the level of their fellows. It is no accident that a television consumer programme is called *Fair Go*. It has been top-rated since it began in 1977, waging war against scams, cons and bureaucracy.

The Fair Go principle was at work when New Zealand became the first country in the world (in 1893) to grant women the right to vote. Some Kiwi blokes suggest that the country has been going downhill ever since. The women who now hold all of the country's highest political offices know that, on the contrary, things have never been better.

New Zealand was also one of the first countries to establish an office of Race Relations Conciliator. Part of its function is to provide explanations to the majority of how the minorities feel when they and their perceived customs are at the receiving end of jokes. Kiwis approve of this. They are wedded to the Fair Go principle, but they also like to laugh. The result is that the Race Relations Conciliator has driven much humour underground, where it flourishes, usually affectionately, but with a sharp edge if imposed political correctness is involved. Kiwis do not like to be told how to think.

Everyone places fair dealing and social justice at the top of the ladder of virtues – even when dealing with Aussies. After all, every kindergarten child knows this riddle:

Q: How can you tell an Aussie?
A: You can't tell an Aussie anything.

The Aussies are not seen as the world's best sports, so are fair game for taunting and teasing, especially about certain of their cricketing techniques. No-one is willing to forget the occasion when, with one ball remaining in a one-day cricket match in which New Zealand had a last crucial chance to even the score, an Aussie bowled underarm. Fair's fair, but there are limits.

This is why the Kiwis didn't altogether approve of the tactics of an advertising copywriter who, to push one of New Zealand's beers on the Australian market, capitalised on the fate of an Aussie yacht that broke in half and sank during an America's Cup race. The snappy caption to a full-page ad for the beer declared, 'There's only one thing that goes down faster than an Aussie yacht.'

The Kiwis enjoyed the joke, and then helped their rivals to equip a new boat. Funny yes – but even the Aussies deserve a Fair Go.

Behaviour

Understatement

Kiwis tend to deprecate that which they value most. They hate to 'make a fuss' or otherwise draw attention to themselves. "Not bad, eh", said of an achievement, is the very essence of pride. To show off, or 'skite', is to invite universal mockery and condemnation. To say of someone, "He likes the sound of his own voice," is to damn indeed.

A good Kiwi bloke plays things down and does not stand on ceremony. The rugby player who scores a try is no longer expected to look as if he is bravely accepting a death sentence, but other than in sport, emotion is not something to be shown in public, and not much in private either. A blokess is allowed more latitude. She is even expected by men to 'carry on a bit'.

Television likes tears: "If it weeps, shoot it" is the Kiwi TV journalists' maxim, but interviewers can have a hard time whipping up any semblance of emotion. A fireman emerging, blackened, from an inferno with a rescued child in his arms might allow to the camera that it was "A bit hot in there". If two cars are nearly demolished in a collision and the two drivers are able to limp away, one might say to the other, "That was close."

The Chopping Down Reflex

A Kiwi works on the premise that if it's taller than you are, chop it down. This applied to the original bush which covered the land and dwarfed the new settlers. In fact, so successful were they that huge areas became denuded and are now having to be re-clothed in man-made forest.

People feel that those who may think themselves superior, especially if they return home trailing clouds of glory acquired overseas, are asking to be chopped down to everyone else's level. This cultural trait is referred to locally as 'tall poppy syndrome', as in, it's the tallest poppy that's the first one to get its head lopped off. An exception to this rule is Sir Edmund Hillary. When he and Sherpa Tensing were the first to climb Mount Everest and there was all that commotion, the knives could have been readied back home. But Hillary showed he was just a good average Kiwi simply ticking something off his list of things to do, as it were, when on his return to base camp, he said, "We knocked the bastard off." Everyone could go along with that.

Politeness

Informality is the trademark of the Kiwi. Standing on ceremony is greeted with raised eyebrows. Anything that is seen as pretentious, stuffy or over-elaborate is despised. Yet politeness is valued and expected at all ages and stages. Failing to acknowledge one of Mum's old school friends on the street, for instance, will be certain to have repercussions. There are so few people in New Zealand that everyone knows everyone else, or is related to, or at least a neighbour of someone you might know. Any lapse in manners is bound to be 'sheeted' home, and thus swiftly known by one and all.

Kiwis can carry politeness to considerable lengths. Someone who has been served with a cup of coffee may say to a waitress, "Excuse me, sorry, but may I have a teaspoon please?" If this were the U.S., the startled waitress would ask, "Where you from, honey?" In New

13

Zealand she would say, "Sure, sorry, here you go." 'Sorry' is the universal shorthand, the coinage of good manners, said by both people if they bump into each other in the street.

People working in businesses and services involved in tourism are urged to enrol in the KiwiHost course, a practical workshop with an emphasis on friendly hospitality, understanding visitors' needs, and general helpfulness. To Kiwis, politeness is synonymous with warmth and generosity of spirit. Thus North Islanders, when complimented by visitors on their scenery, will ask anxiously, "But have you seen the South Island yet?" They do not want to be seen as hogging the best bits for themselves.

The Kiwis expect and value what they call 'decent' behaviour. Mild eccentricity sticks out and is therefore embarrassing. Conformity is king in small towns. Kiwi women are still close enough to pioneering life (or its traditions) to know that, in theory, 'girls can do anything' – and do. Yet, until not so very long ago strict standards of feminine propriety required a lady to wear a hat and gloves in public and not draw attention to herself. Now only the gloves remain – for winter warmth.

'Bloody', the great Australian expletive, is frequently used, but not often in public places. Big hoardings in Australia do not mince their words when it comes to important messages. In Victoria, for instance, a safe driving campaign was highly successful when roadsides bloomed with exhortations 10 feet high: 'If you drink and drive you're a bloody fool.' Greatly daring, Kiwi road safety authorities borrowed the idea, and now television ads speak, still comparatively mildly, of 'bloody idiots'.

Parliament, at one time the home of the robust denunciation and few-holds-barred debate, has become almost polite. An old-time Labour MP was once accused of profiteering and acquiring great holdings in timber. He jumped to his feet and declared that he "didn't own enough timber to build a shithouse for a cockroach". The conservative character of the Kiwi Parliament was revealed when the negative reaction to his uncivil language became an even bigger story than his apparent swindle.

The Big O.E.

For many years, New Zealand was thought by younger Kiwis to be a sleepy backwater. Disillusioned fledglings would flee its shores for their 'Big O.E.' (Overseas Experience) as a way of escaping the stifling influences of provincialism and distance from the world. Few people were surprised by the quip that New Zealand is where novelists send characters they don't know what to do with.

At its peak, so many Kiwi graduates were flying off without a return ticket that the O.E. was called a 'brain drain'. It was anthropologist Margaret Mead who declared that New Zealand's role was "to send forth its bright young men and women to run the rest of the world". This tradition helped some countries more than others. A Kiwi prime minister once remarked trenchantly of a gadfly critic of his who left to live in Australia, that his departure had raised the average I.Q. of both countries.

The O.E. remains a rite of passage – a way for young Kiwis to learn about the world and gain some perspective on their homeland. But increasingly they fly back to the nest after some time away, safe in the knowledge that they're returning to just about the best place on the planet. New Zealand may be geographically remote, but, in an age of easy global travel and communication, Kiwis no longer consider themselves isolated.

Conversation

The average Kiwi (particularly the average Kiwi bloke) is a person of few words. Dragging conversation from a Kiwi bloke can cause those unfamiliar with the New Zealand male to break into a cold sweat. The only sure way to loosen a Kiwi bloke's tongue is to lure him into a bar and then throw out a barbed comment about the current form of the New Zealand rugby team, the All Blacks. This will almost invariably give rise to a mumbled diatribe against the current coaching staff and a screed on "the worrying decline in forward pack dominance".

Among Kiwi women, the most frequently used couple of words are 'you know', said with a rising inflection. Nobody is actually expected to know. It is just a useful filler while thinking of what to say. Families hold competitions to see who can bag the most 'you know's' uttered in news interviews or talk shows.

Despite typically having little to say for themselves, Kiwis feel awkward if they sit or stand next to someone for any length of time and do not talk. This is a brazen reversal of the British habit of keeping oneself to oneself and can be blamed on the newness of New Zealand. There were so few people in the country for so many years that the first hardy types had to talk to themselves or they would have forgotten how. Their excitement when they encountered another human in the wilderness naturally caused them to utter – nothing fancy, you know, just "Gidday" or "How yuh doing?", the great Kiwi ice-breakers.

A standard topic of conversation between Kiwis flows smoothly and safely from and to the weather. Any change in the previous few days' temperature becomes that day's greetings. "Hot enough for you?" or "Cold enough for you?" The changes are rung with "Sunny enough?", "Wet enough?", and so forth.

There is continuous lip-service to optimism: whether or

not there is a need to worry about something, the oblig-ing Kiwis tell one another that it will be "good as gold", "right as rain" and "no prob" (problem), usually quali-fied by one of those great reassurers in any situation, "She'll be right", or "Piece of cake".

They are also the world's best grumblers. Recent English immigrants are about the only people who say, "Mustn't grumble" and then go right ahead and grumble. Everyone else just grumbles. Keeping up a stream of good-natured grumbling directed at politicians, weather forecasters, the economy, and anyone getting too big for his boots is the custom of the country.

Kiwis encountered when you are at the beach, in the street or sharing public transport, like to be asked for advice: it gives them the chance to be friendly and help-ful. The farther south you go, the friendlier the people. Maybe it's because they are lonelier. Those people waving from a roadside on the remote West Coast, for instance, are unlikely to be flagging you down for help. They are just enjoying a moment of contact.

Attitudes and Values

The Kiwi Class System

Kiwi society is composed of three main groups and a self-labelled elite, all with strong feelings about the way they see themselves. Sensitive New Age Kiwis (SNAKS) are found in urban areas (particularly Auckland) and in lifestyle blocks on the outskirts of towns. Traditional Old-fashioned Rural Kiwis (TORKS) are out in the rest of the country. Among them are 'rednecks' – the ultra-conservative small farm holders, and almost equally con-servative business people determined to keep what they've got – who frequently form the majority in Parliament and on local bodies. The Māori, particularly the younger generation, are increasingly seen as Independently Willed Indigenous Kiwis (IWIKS).

Kiwi class distinctions, say the educated, are based more on education than on money or belonging to old families. Better Educated New Zealanders (BENZERS) regard themselves as the elite and look down on most SNAKS (as being foolishly trendy), nearly all TORKS (for obvious reasons), and some but by no means all IWIKS.

BENZERS are a minority. Asians are correct when they perceive that Kiwis do not place education high in the scheme of things. BENZERS would never dream of calling themselves, or others, 'Kiwis'. They regard the word merely as a vulgar device to fit the label New Zealanders into a headline. In this attitude they are hopelessly in the minority.

Some TORKS have aspirations to become SNAKS, whereas some SNAKS are reverting to type and becoming TORKS when confronted by the demands of radical IWIKS. An IWIK can also be a SNAK, TORK or BENZER.

TORKS like to see themselves as the rightful contenders in the struggle to secure the world's main agricultural markets although, as farms amalgamate and become more mechanised, there are far fewer farmers than there used to be. SNAKS, with some extra-sensitive reservations about the growing gap between the haves and have-nots, consider they are part of the global community, and to the fore in terms of economic and societal growth. IWIKS see themselves as a sovereign people. BENZERS believe the other groupings would see the light if only they were better educated.

The one thing they have in common is that they all regard themselves as rugged pioneers capable of fixing anything with a piece of number eight fencing wire (the country's staple tool since pioneering days), and perfectly able, most of the time, to take on the rest of the world at anything, particularly sport.

Family Life

Strongly bonded family loyalty is seen as the backbone of Kiwi society. This is especially true for the Māori and Pacific Island peoples, with their tradition of the large extended family unit.

The marriage rate for the entire country is reducing year by year but, for those who do, the age at first marriage is 28 for women and 30 for men. Despite the growing maturity of those taking the plunge, the divorce rate is also rising. A period of two years of formal separation is sufficient grounds for divorce, with no need for the peccadilloes of either partner to be aired in the courts.

Though cohabitation and solo parenthood are on the increase, romance is far from dead. Mothers still plan a traditional white (or off-white) wedding for their daughters, with bridesmaids, reception and honeymoon – the whole works. Blokes generally leave them to it, and hope for the best.

It is relatively common among Māori and Polynesians for children to be looked after solely by a grandparent or other older guardian. This may have worked well in the former, highly organised, tribal societies but, with most Māori now living in towns and cities, far from their tribal bases, it is becoming increasingly hard for grandparents in isolation to catch up on and cope with all the changes that children accept as a matter of course.

At the other end of life, granny flats are popular, but most elderly Kiwis prefer living independently while they can. A growth industry is the rest home, the 'Peacehavens', where the frail elderly can go, some by choice in order not to be a burden on their families, others because they have nobody willing or able to look after them. Māori and Pacific Island peoples are conspicuously absent from this last group. Honouring the aged is part of their cultures.

By 2050 the over 65s are expected to account for 25%

of the Kiwi population. Many of today's older generation choose to live on a quiet stretch of New Zealand's ample coast. There, they can comfortably play the role of 'silver surfers' – hitting the waves in the morning, and using the internet to keep on top of world events in the afternoon.

Religion

The pioneering *Pakeha* settlers were mainly Protestant, and Protestant values still largely hold sway (though not necessarily to the extent of actual church attendance). Most *Pakeha*, if pushed to name their religion, will say Church of England (Anglican), Presbyterian, Roman Catholic or Methodist, the faiths of their founding fathers.

Methodism is strong among many Pacific Island groups. The Church of the Latter Day Saints (Mormons) and Jehovah's Witnesses also claim a share of primarily Māori adherents. Faith is often a matter of which missionary got there first.

The religion that unites all Kiwis, though, is rugby. Nothing raises religious fervour in a Kiwi like a closely-fought match particularly if the All Blacks are playing one of their traditional rivals – South Africa, Australia, or England. Saturday is the traditional day of worship. On any given Saturday throughout the winter months, Kiwis of all stripes can be found sitting before make-shift shrines in their living rooms or local pubs, staring intently and screaming intermittently at their television sets.

Despite the country's fervour for rugby, Kiwi faith, it must be said, has taken a bit of a hit in recent years. Before the beginning of the professional era in rugby, the All Blacks routinely swept aside all other teams on the international rugby stage. Any All Blacks' loss was mourned as a national tragedy, and was typically accompanied by a downswing in the local stock index, an upsurge in anti-social behaviour, and a countrywide depression.

However, in recent years, other rugby-playing nations have managed to lift their play to something approaching the All Blacks' standards and Kiwis are having to accept that their national team will be beaten on a regular basis. Of course, an old guard of religious zealots remains, ready to crucify their team for any blunder. In the months before and during the 4-yearly rugby world cup, the All Blacks' coaching staff is scrutinised and criticised more exhaustively than prospective candidates for a new Pope.

Obsessions

The Weather

The weather is the Kiwi's number one obsession.

New Zealand sits plumb in the middle of the ocean and thousands of kilometres from any other substantial land mass. This explains its unique vegetation and wildlife and is also why it is so hard for meteorologists to predict what kind of weather is going to reach what part of the country. Bad weather, of course, always comes over the ditch from Australia.

The media cash in on this preoccupation by trying to make personalities out of the forecasters. The forecasters themselves, when saying that the weather will be fine, have taken to hedging their bets. They will say, for instance, that there's a 15% chance they could be wrong.

Students of journalism are given special tuition in handling weather stories and the ramifications, social and economic, of long stretches of either drought or storm. They are never short of copy. The windstorm which lifted a 21-stone policeman clean off his feet was unusual only because it occurred in Auckland. Inhabitants of Wellington are used to having to hang on to lampposts to save themselves from being blown away.

There is one constant. The nation's farmers are never satisfied with what they get and even less satisfied with the forewarnings. They never believe them, anyway. And who can blame them? El Niño has wrought considerable damage, and floods in some areas and droughts in others have now given farmers something substantial to grumble about. Global warming and the depletion of the ozone layer have even become topics in the pub.

Since everyone has to take account of dramatic daily weather changes when planning work or leisure activities (a torrential downpour for five solid hours can make a difference to your day), in many households the peak-hour radio and television forecasts are listened to with almost religious intensity. It is not done to telephone someone at such times.

Sport (see Religion)

Running the weather a close second in the obsession stakes is sport in all its manifestations. The match of the day, the day of the match, the player of the day, the week, the year – in every conceivable sport the drums of publicity beat for ever more heroes. Role models for the young come almost exclusively from the sporting arena. Whenever there is a world contest and the Kiwis are likely to win, everyone, male and female, young and old, settles in rapt concentration round their radio and television sets.

In a poll organised by New Zealand's post office, which aimed to feature the most famous Kiwis in each of several categories on a series of stamps, the sports category alone had 83 Kiwi contenders. The fact that there were only a meagre 18 in the section for community leaders and social campaigners (in a country renowned for social crusading) is no doubt because the pollsters, all true Kiwis, knew a lot about sports people but not so much about anyone else.

Politics

Another obsession is with politics and politicians. Kiwis like to think they are politically well informed. They should be: they are fed a constant stream of political news, anecdotes and personality pieces – barrels enough to fuel their sessions over their beer.

Any political scandal looms large because there is a surprising degree of probity among elected representatives. In Australia politicians are routinely called 'scumbags', quite often with cause. New Zealand, by contrast, consistently comes close to the top of world rankings that measure levels of public integrity. In New Zealand the worst that can be said about many politicians is that they're boring or irrelevant.

But lack of personality is no hindrance to humour. The nation rocked with laughter when two senior and avowedly redneck politicians were caught out in a joke that misfired. The then Minister of Tourism was running a weekly radio talkback show not noted for its sensitivity. A caller with an exaggerated Māori intonation who said his name was Hone (Māori for John) and that he was unemployed, made it plain he wasn't interested in finding a job because life was much easier on the dole. In other words he was that despised creature, the dole-bludger*. But a journalist recognised the voice and exposed the caller as none other than the friend and colleague of the Minister of Tourism – the Senior Government Whip. Politicians in New Zealand have no tradition of honourable resignation. They don't go unless they are pushed. The Senior Government Whip, alias Hone, was made to resign his post (though remaining an MP) as a direct result of the public uproar. The majority clearly agreed that the Māori should not be insulted in this way,

* To 'bludge' or to get something for nothing, and to which you're not entitled anyway, is about as low as you can go.

while continuing to chuckle. Kiwis have always believed in having a bet both ways.

Animals

The nation's economy was built (and remains heavily reliant) on farm animals, so it is not surprising that animal welfare is high on the list of Kiwi concerns. Under a law which allows a referendum to be held when enough signatures to a petition have been gathered, one of the first crusades was to ban the practice of rearing battery hens. Parliament, not to be outwitted, had framed the legislation so that it was not bound to pass any result into law. Everyone knew this, but signed the petition all the same, to let the politicians know that chicken welfare deserves a place on the political agenda.

This obsession with the welfare of animals can extend even to a species foreign to the country. New Zealand has no snakes, and definitely wants to keep it that way, but when a baby boa constrictor was intercepted in a freight container and duly put down, feelings were such that a prime time television news reader was moved to say comfortingly that it had been frozen, "and freezing for a boa is a gentle way to die".

Horses are the number one favourite animal. Many children, especially girls, are horse-mad and beg to belong to pony clubs. If it were not so hard to keep horses in a quarter-acre section, they might even outnumber the nation's cats and dogs, though not, of course, the sheep.

After the government ordered the culling of thousands of wild horses which were killing rare native flora in the bush it had to do an about-turn, and was forced to have many of them captured and offered to the public to care for. Trophies at international horse events are regularly carried off by Kiwi riders. But, of course, the best place for a horse is on the race course and first past the post.

The TAB (Totalisator Agency Board, or betting shop) is handily placed in every urban centre. It's not for nothing that 'you bet' is Kiwi for a very firm 'yes'.

Hunting and Pest Control

In its primal state New Zealand had practically no native creatures except birds and seals. All others have been imported. Even pests such as wasps are not indigenous, and there are no poisonous creatures except for a very rarely seen native spider, the katipo.

Hunting is an obsession, and a variety of species of deer was introduced for sport. They soon multiplied to the point where deer cullers had to be employed, tough outback men who created their own mythology. The Department of Conservation, or DOC, wants to see the bush free from the ravages of deer. The Deer Stalkers Association and those with tourism interests see the situation differently. The Kiwis began deer farming when they discovered that other nations would pay high prices for the various parts of the deer, from the meat to the supposedly aphrodisiac velvet.

Two unfortunate animals have no claim to national sympathy and are obsessively hunted down – rabbits, which came from Britain, and possums, from Australia, which gobble up pastures and bush. The possum population is now in excess of 70 million and poses a real threat to native forests. Keen gardeners are also concerned by the possums' partiality to orchards, roses and vegetables. Government schemes for poisoning and trapping almost keep up with the birth rate, but long-term hopes for control are pinned on family planning measures – the Pill for possums.

One entrepreneur had the bright idea of giving possums the name of 'Kiwi bears' in an attempt to sell the meat – a not-very-exciting cross between chicken and rabbit.

Few have been fooled.

Furry corpses found flattened on country roads invariably are possums. Rabbits are far too crafty: many even managed to dodge the controversially introduced RCV (a viral disease equivalent to myxomatosis). The Kiwi who wants to clinch an argument with someone he regards as a naïve idealist propounding a hopeless cause will say, "You'll never catch the last rabbit."

Leisure and Pleasure

Sport is the Kiwi's main leisure interest. This means following broadcasts, going to watch, and taking part – in that order. The main sporting preoccupations of the Kiwi bloke have always been rugby, horse racing and cricket, and for Kiwi women, netball is the sport of choice. Race meetings continue to draw crowds. The performance of the Kiwi cricket team, however, has been so inconsistent in recent years that lawn bowls is starting to challenge cricket in the TV ratings.

The Kiwi sporting public is a fickle one. Success is met with (understated) adulation, but failure is accompanied by the sound of sharpening knives.

Yachting

Because New Zealand is a long skinny country of three main islands, nobody lives far from the sea. It's no surprise the Kiwis excel at yachting. They start young: children can easily get to a lake or the sea and learn to sail a dinghy, and it's better to have them out in a boat in all that healthy fresh air than underfoot at home when you are busy watching sport on television or getting on with your DIY.

Nothing gave the Kiwis as much pleasure as winning the world's premier yachting trophy, the America's Cup, twice running. The fact that New Zealand could play David to the American Goliath with all their space age resources was a great boost to national pride.

The disgust of the losers was succinctly expressed by Eric Sharp, an American journalist: 'The United States invented the space shuttle, the atomic bomb and Disneyland. We have 35 times more land than New Zealand, 80 times the population, 144 times the gross national product... our 10 biggest metropolises each have more people than all of New Zealand... So how come a superpower got routed in the America's Cup, the world's most technically oriented yacht race, by a country of 3.5 million that outproduces us only in sheep manure?'

While the Americans went home to lick their wounds, half a million Kiwis (more than one-eighth of the entire population) converged on the cities to welcome the yachties home. Offices and schools closed, ticker tape and balloons filled the air, and strong Kiwis dashed tears from their eyes. It was as if the whole country had just won the national lottery. "You played fair," said the welcoming Governor-General, and others declared it was just like conquering Everest all over again.

Team New Zealand lost their second defence of the America's Cup to a team representing Switzerland (a land-locked country). The bitter taste of defeat was made worse by the fact that many of those sailing on the Swiss yacht, including the helmsman and the tactician, were Kiwis, who had defected from Team New Zealand. Disappointed patriots were quite sure that this was not a Fair Go, but found some solace in pointing out to anyone who would listen that it was a group of Kiwis who ended up winning the cup, even though the win was for a rival nation.

DIY

The Kiwis grow up expecting they will Do It Themselves. "Piece of cake," they say. There is nothing for a Kiwi like the triumph of fixing, enlarging, remodelling and building from scratch. Unwary visitors are taken on tours of inspection, both inside the home and out. Hardware stores and garden centres do booming business at weekends when Kiwis, recuperating from a week's work, hurl themselves into the frantic activity of DIY. In the evenings they relax by watching home improvement programmes on television.

Gardening is high on the list of weekend occupations. It, too, is tackled headlong so that the utmost can be wrung out of every spare moment. Gardens used to be divided strictly on gender lines. He did the vegetables, she the flowers. The women's movement counts among its significant gains the fact that most gardens are now unisex (i.e., she does everything, while he watches the rugby). Towns and suburbs have garden competitions, and flower shows great and small are regular proof that almost anything grows bigger and better in New Zealand. Disbelievers are directed to study the hills of golden gorse and broom, importees from Britain which flourish so well in the benign Kiwi climate that they have had to be declared noxious weeds.

For men, work on the car is its own reward. A Kiwi bloke's car is a source of immense pride, and in many cases is kept around long past its use-by date in order to justify the existence of a shed (another basic staple of Kiwi male life). Kiwi blokes live by a series of strict rules when it comes to their cars. A bloke's car should not be an automatic anything, must be a V-something (preferably 8), have space to carry a couple of crates of beer and up to a dozen mates, and should smell at all times like the farm or rugby club (meaning no little pine-tree things hanging from the rear-view mirror). Any lesser car is only fit to be driven by suits on the grid-locked motorways of Auckland.

Even though a quantity of barely-used cars are imported from Japan, many vehicles on the road are so old they look like escapees from a vintage car museum. It is not just sentiment which makes people regard their 'rust buckets' as others do their faithful horses put out to grass. They can improvise and cajole a longer working life out of their cars than virtually anyone else.

For women, DIY extends to catering. The words 'Ladies a plate', as part of the notice of a function, have a long history. Catering is usually a shared enterprise, especially in rural areas, with women competing to bring along plates bearing the most impressive fare. Stories abound of newcomers to the country who take the notice at face value and arrive at a social function with half a dozen plates tucked under their arms, in the belief that the organisers are short of crockery.

At that perennial small town fund raiser, the cake stall, the great Kiwi cake is the eight-inch-high sponge sandwich, feather-light, dusted with icing sugar and joined together with raspberry jam and dollops of thick sweetened cream. The Heart Foundation just has to look the other way.

Arts and Leisure Festivals

A rapidly spreading event in many parts of New Zealand is the annual learning festival with workshops in the arts and activities such as sailing and kayaking. These have grown out of the new economic emphasis on helping yourself and not looking to the state for succour. You can learn to paint, sail a yacht or write a novel, all for a charge which is ridiculously small – especially if your novel becomes a bestseller.

Small towns make capital out of their local attractions.

Highly individual and well-patronised festivals result, bringing a boost to local economies. For instance, Bulls, a junction township named after a pioneer settler, decided it might as well capitalise on all the jokes about its name. Virtually all its businesses renamed themselves. A café is called Delect-a-bull, an antiques and souvenir business is Collect-a-bull. Need a money machine? Go to the Cash-a-bull. Firemen are Extinguish-a-bulls and cops, Const-a-bulls. The public loos are Relieve-a-bulls, and if people feel they need absolution they go to the local church, Forgive-a-bull. The citizens are waiting for their population to justify a family planning clinic. It will, of course, be Inconceive-a-bull.

Other places have promoted new sports such as gum-boot throwing or kiwifruit chucking to give themselves a distinctive character. And for tourists to Rotorua, there are beauty contests for sheep in which the sheep take the stage all fluffed up, primped and perfumed. Throughout the country, competing and self-betterment committees thrive. They have a long history – a group of early settlers, stumped for something exciting to do in their rare leisure time, formed themselves into an Egg-Laying Competition Committee.

Sense of Humour

The Kiwis love to laugh, particularly at politicians and any others silly enough to set themselves up as knowing what's best for everyone else. This is why they enjoy out-witting bureaucrats. A winemaker wanted to excavate a hillside behind his premises to make a wine cellar, but was refused a building permit. He gave the matter some thought, applied instead for a mining permit, and now big wooden doors set in the hillside lead connoisseurs and tourists into his 'wine mine'.

Kiwis are quick to pounce. One prime minister, universally seen as somewhat pompous, was rash enough to agree to address a student rally together with the leader of the opposition on whose side the students soon showed themselves to be. The prime minister was asked a question, pondered, then articulated slowly, "I — don't — think...", whereupon the whole audience roared as one, "You never think!" Another prime minister, noted for his one-liners, was demolishing America's foreign policy at an Oxford Union debate. When his American opponent trotted out the line that the nuclear bomb was essential to world peace, this Kiwi brought the house down on his side by declaring, "I can smell the uranium on your breath."

Much of the humour is home-grown. *Pakeha* and Māori used to make good-humoured jokes about each other, but the imported doctrine of political correctness has had an inhibiting effect. These days people are inclined to tiptoe around, afraid of giving offence. They long for another Billy T. James, the Māori comedian who used to make genial fun of Māori and *Pakeha* alike. Billy thrived on sending up race relations and other Kiwi rivalries. When a radical Māori woman said, "Kill a white and be a hero!", Billy said plaintively, "What about all us half-castes? Do we just get wounded or something?" And of himself he said: "I'm half Māori and half Scots. Half of me wants to go to the pub and get pissed, and the other half doesn't want to pay for it."

Asked what they laugh at most, the Kiwis' response is near-unanimous – "Australians!" Endless Aussie jokes are told with great good cheer in the full knowledge that Aussie humour has Kiwis as the butt.

Q: What do you call a field full of Aussies?
A: A vacant lot.

Q: What do you call an Aussie with half a brain?
A: Gifted.

Q: What's the difference between an Aussie wedding and an Aussie funeral?
A: At the funeral there is one fewer drunk.

Kiwis know that Aussies have a predilection for maligning them with jokes about sheep and therefore have one or two of their own – the difference being that Kiwis consider their jokes about Aussies contain a troubling grain of truth. For example:

The Aussies have just discovered a new use for sheep. Wool.

One Kiwi comedian, John Clark, who has gone so far as to exile himself to Australia (so as to develop more elaborate ways of 'taking the piss' out of the Aussies), returns periodically to give Kiwis the lowdown on doings trans-Tasman. He dresses for performances in black singlet and gumboots, and his yarns are country-style leisurely and in accord with his stage name, which is Fred Dagg. Dags are those pieces of manure-encrusted wool that adorn the backside of sheep. In the Kiwi system of inverted humour, it is something of a compliment to be called "a bit of a dag" – it means others are amused by your antics and admire you. And when Kiwis want someone to hurry up and get a move on, they say, "C'mon! Rattle your dags!".

Kiwis have a good line in gallows humour, for example:

A Kiwi was caught on camera exceeding the speed limit. The morning post brought a demand for payment of $100 together with an incriminating photograph of his car. Next day the traffic police received an envelope containing their demand with a photograph of two $50 bills. In response, the Kiwi received the same demand along with a photograph of a pair of handcuffs.

The battle of the sexes provides plenty of fodder for Kiwi comedians:

A Kiwi bloke left work on Friday afternoon and instead of going home he chose to spend the entire weekend with his mates. When he finally arrived home late on Sunday night he was met at the door by his very irate wife. She nagged him for hours about his irresponsible actions, then demanded: 'How would you like it if you didn't see me for two whole days?', to which the bloke replied, 'Suits me fine!'

Monday went by and he didn't see his wife.

Tuesday went by and he still didn't see his wife.

On Wednesday the swelling went down just enough that he could glimpse her out of the corner of one eye.

Tucker and Grog

Kiwis have always grown the plentiful quantities of the healthiest food, but the early settlers stayed true to their British roots by stewing, boiling, or otherwise frazzling all of the flavour and goodness out of anything to be placed on their tables. Old habits of over-cooking die hard and it is still possible to find soggy greens, but a great food revolution has swept the land, and fully fledged foodies at last have their place in the sun.

Cook books regularly top the best-seller lists. Prime-time television has a daily 'good food' demonstration. Even the loneliest little provincial town may offer eateries where the menu features such delights as 'tempura-coated nori-encased salmon and pirouettes with a blueberry and tamarillo coulis'. The young, having travelled and tasted in the capitals of the world, have spearheaded the change in eating habits, and the demands of tourism, grandly known as the hospitality industry, have led to five-star cookery courses throughout the land.

More than a thousand young chefs, waiters, somme-liers, bar-people and baristas (as coffee-making experts like to be called) compete each year for the hospitality industry's most prestigious awards at the New Zealand Culinary Fare. What is said to be the world's largest 'hot kitchen' is set up at Auckland's Expo Centre, and the dishes prepared there dazzle the eye as well as the palate.

As for grog, since the early 1980s the country has been transformed from a footnote in the catalogue of the world's wines into one of the leading chapters. The white wines in particular regularly win gold medals on the international stage. These days, the toughest, bluffest Kiwi joker could hold forth on "a cheeky little sauvignon blanc with subtle, mouth-filling flavours with just a hint of fig, all combined with a clean, crisp finish".

Were it not for New Zealand's relatively small production, wine might be as much a part of mealtimes in every home as it is in France. But only 'might': the Kiwi drink from pioneering days has been, and still is, beer. Beer is the great thirst-quencher, the sporting drink, and is still what 'the boys' rush into the pub for. In the far south, however, where the early settlers from Scotland put a lasting brand on the country, the question to a guest is not "What'll you drink?" but "Will you have anything in your Scotch?"

Kai

Māori place names often commemorate food. *Kai* means food or a meal, and *koura* is crayfish, so the town of Kaikoura, base for watching whales and dolphins, means great tucker, or dining on the best.

Most families regularly tuck in to fish and chips – fresh and surpassingly good if bought in a coastal town – but the roast dinner remains the all-time favourite. The older male Kiwi is still suspicious of new-fangled foods such as quiche or pasta. He, and indeed most of the family, are at their happiest when served roast lamb, gravy and mint sauce, with roast potatoes, parsnips, pumpkin and *kumara*, the Māori name for the delicious sweet potato.

The standard salad that older Kiwis remember from childhood made of one-variety lettuce cut up hours earlier and decorated with slices of tomato, cucumber and hard-boiled eggs is a thing of the past. There has been an explosion of experimentation with salads. Fed by interest in vegetarianism, platters boast crisp salad vegetables presented with fresh fruits and garnished with herbs and your choice of smoked salmon, fat mussels and a range of gourmet cheeses. Olive and avocado oils and exotic vinegars are now everyday ingredients.

The traditional festive pudding is the cream-covered pavlova or 'pav', an airy concoction of meringue and cream named after the great Russian ballet dancer, lavishly decorated with slices of lime-green kiwifruit. A good pav recipe is a must for any Kiwi woman. An old saying runs "You'll never get a husband unless you can make a good pav…"

The production of a pav, though, is beyond the capability of the average male Kiwi. Pavs have an uncanny knack of sensing a bloke's discomfort in the kitchen and responding by self-destructing. Instead of emerging from the oven as a thing of beauty and sweetness, a bloke's pav is likely to have collapsed under its own weight into a sludgy pile of congealing liquid stickiness. The only safe recipe that blokes have discovered for pav goes something like this:

1. Take a few dollars from the beer kitty.
2. Drive to the local supermarket.
3. Shell out for a pav and a bottle of cream (remembering to grab a 6-pack of the regional brew on the way to the checkout).
4. Return home, prepare the cream and spread it over the purchased pav to give it that 'look what I just whipped up' appearance.
5. Open a beer, watch some rugby, and later, enjoy the compliments of housemates impressed by such a display of culinary expertise.

Kiwifruit are another New Zealand staple. This furry produce did not originate in New Zealand but, like so many imports, flourish in its adopted climate. In the early 1960s an exporter wanted to market them in the United States, but he had a problem. Those were the years of the Cold War and extreme suspicion in the U.S. of anything remotely pertaining to communism. Since New Zealanders had always known the fruit as 'Chinese gooseberries', such self-professed 'Commie fruit' could not enter the American market. What to do? An advertising agency was asked to come up with a list of possible new names. Name number 30 was 'kiwiberry'. The exporter pounced on it, but consulted a botanist who said, 'It's not a berry, it's a fruit', and so kiwifruit was born – though for the purpose of distinction, now that they are grown around the world, New Zealand-grown kiwifruit are marketed under the label 'Zespri'.

There is one staple of Kiwi cuisine it will take a lot to dislodge and that is the bottle of tomato sauce. Every household has this indispensable bright red bottle on the pantry shelf. It may not be used so much these days, but it's there in case, for the custom of the country has always been to add 'tom' sauce to everything – with the possible exception of pavlova.

What Is Sold Where

New Zealand long retained many of its customs and traditions from the other side of the world and from its pioneering days. Little was sold on a Saturday, and nothing on Sunday, causing British food writer Clement Freud (in a broadside widely reported, of course) to say that he had visited New Zealand but that it 'seemed to be shut'.

'Saturday opening' was a hard-fought battle. Village shops were run by the community, and churches and trade unions maintained it would mean the end of family life if

Mum had to serve behind a counter on Saturdays. As usual, pragmatism and opportunism won the day. Now it's 'open slather' (a free-for-all) in tourist centres every day of the week. In urban areas supermarkets, DIY stores and garden centres have introduced enthusiastic Kiwis to a new commercial age of all-day-every-day shopping, and in the rest of the country smaller shops sell madly on Saturday mornings to make up for the lost years.

Even the smallest village has at least one 'dairy'. Dairies are the country's convenience stores, selling milk, butter and practically everything else. In some parts of the country milk is still delivered to the door in glass bottles, but plastic and cardboard containers are increasingly used, and give rise to clamour about wasted resources and waste disposal.

You can find pretty well everything at the petrol stations – a range of snacks and basic foods as well as car and handyman accessories, and even materials for home renovation. They'll always have a steady stream of customers ready to Give It a Go.

Custom and Tradition

Holidays

The Christmas holidays are the most important time for the family-centred Kiwis. 'Going home for Christmas' to parents and grandparents is the rule rather than the exception, and the summer holiday break lasts from around Christmas to the end of January, when the children go back to school.

Christmas falls in high summer but this is not seen as sufficient reason for departing from the old English-style Christmas dinner of hot roast turkey and all the traditional trimmings. The odd, daring cook tries to change the menu to suit the temperature, but it's never the same.

Other imported Christmas traditions extend to dragging a tree into the house and decorating it with lights and baubles. Some Kiwis have even picked up on the American custom of decorating the outsides of their homes with all manner of flashing lights and glittering plastic. Although these displays are ostensibly for the benefit of children, the fact that the sun doesn't set until around 9 p.m. during the summer months means that visiting these decorated homes is very much a late-night affair.

It is not always as much a pleasure as a tradition when tents and sleeping bags and holiday gear are packed into cars along with the children and the pets, and the long drive begins, often from one end of the country to the other. Many people have their own favoured holiday spots where they camp or stay in 'baches' (originally bachelors' quarters of minimum comfort) by lakes, rivers, and sea. As hardly anyone is at their own home, Christmas and the month of January are great times to rent a vacant house for a few weeks.

Time spent driving around New Zealand does not amount to 'travel' for a Kiwi. Crossing the ditch to Australia, a three-hour journey, scarcely counts. Only escaping to the South Pacific (a flight of a dozen hours or more) constitutes real travel.

Homely Habits

In small towns and in the country everyone knows everyone else's business. This is called being neighbourly. Even in the cities people know who their actual neighbours are, and are usually on visiting terms with them. Keeping in touch is a legacy from earliest pioneering days. You kept in touch or you perished.

A constant flow between town and country for visits

and holidays accounts for much of New Zealand's traffic. Most Māori still feel strongly connected to their *marae* (sacred meeting area) back in their tribal heartlands, and many non-Māori are nostalgic for their ancestors' country customs. Those who can afford to revert to pioneering ways have open fireplaces built into their new houses. Real flickering flames give the home a heart, a welcoming centre. This aspect of Kiwi life can come as a shock to visitors used to central heating but Kiwis cling to the idea that they live in a sub-tropical paradise, and even an Antarctic chill inside the house will not dissuade them of this notion. Shivering a bit is a natural part of being hardy. Winter (and even summer), visitors to New Zealand are advised to pack a few extra jumpers for indoor use.

The nation's DIY obsession extends to the exemplary family making their own jams, sauces and chutneys just as their forebears did. They may freeze fruits and vegetables rather than preserve them in glass jars to be placed proudly on pantry shelves, but they are likely to have gathered at least some of the produce from their own garden. No-one would dream of questioning the extra cost in terms of money, effort and time. In this case, a job well done is its own reward.

Farm Rituals

Every shearing time the air becomes heavy with the lanolin smell of fresh creamy fleeces. Good shearers are national heroes, and all shearers must be fed well and at frequent intervals. The women of the farms tote baskets of home-baked buttery scones, cream-filled sponges and heavy fruitcake to the shearing sheds every morning and after-noon 'smoko' time – the old-established workers' tea break which takes place at 10 a.m. and 3 p.m. Fewer shearers now smoke but this simply gives them more time for eating and disposing of gallons of strong tea which they drink in great sweetened gulps.

Smoko fare is just to keep them going between the three cooked meals each day. These begin with the traditional Kiwi farm breakfast of lamb chops, eggs, bacon and potato, the latter fried from the leftovers of the huge pot from the night before.

The sheep farmers, or high country runholders, have been lords of the land almost since European settlement began, certainly since 1882 when refrigerated shipping made lamb exports possible. With government subsidies, they grew as fat as the lambs which rippled down the hillsides in white woolly tides.

These days, sheep numbers are down by more than a third since the mid-1980s, but cattle are making a comeback with the world's recognition that Kiwi beef comes from clean, green pastures. The biggest demand however, is for the country's butter and cheese. (New Zealand supplies the cheese used in McDonald's cheeseburgers throughout the Pacific, as well as Asia, and South America.)

There is now close to one head of cattle per head of population in New Zealand. Between them, these cattle produce over 14 billion litres of milk each year. To reach this sort of output Kiwi farmers have had to become masters of all manner of high-tech machinery. In the slickest operations, up to 350 cows can be milked every hour by a single farmer, using computer-controlled milking machines and revolving cow-carrying carousels. If it wasn't for the constant stream of livestock, these modern milking sheds would bring to mind a cross between an auto assembly line and a carnival ride at the fair.

Farmers have a field-day grumbling. Their suspicion of the government – whichever government it happens to be – is fuelled by what they see as economic manipulation. Subsidies for traditional farming have been swept away, yet there are tax concessions for people who establish forests. This means that grazing land is being gobbled up by radiata pine. To make matters worse, the farmers say, the Johnny-come-latelies who plant these usually aren't farmers at all, just city slickers, paper-shufflers, jokers who have accountants to tell them how to make money. Meanwhile sombre pine trees march by the million over huge chunks of the landscape. At least they're green.

The sweeping pastures offer space, solitude and silence, except, that is, for the singing of the birds, and the moo-ing and maa-ing and baa-ing of the livestock, and sheep-dogs barking if it's mustering time, and the robust language of the musterers. Kiwis accept that a flow of basic Anglo-Saxon (all those short, sharp words) is the only language a Kiwi sheepdog understands – that, and a few borrowings from the Bible. One reason for the great popularity of sheepdog trials on television is that viewers identify and sympathise with the plight of the contestants. When faced with a mob of contrary sheep to get through the hurdles, and no language suitable for public use, how on earth do you get your dog to obey commands? It's a national sport watching and waiting to see if man and beast can safely navigate these perils.

A Solemn Occasion

The year's most solemnly observed day is Anzac Day, on 25th April. The initials stand for Australia New Zealand Army Corps, and the day commemorates the Battle of Gallipoli on the Turkish peninsula on that date in 1915, during the First World War. So many young men lost their lives that the mingled grief and pride of both countries forms an enduring bond.

Anzac Day is when sacrifices in wars throughout the world are remembered. Even the smallest town has its war memorial. From dawn, young and old attend Anzac Day services, the ex-service men and women parading with medals, wreaths and deep solemnity. In the afternoon the mood lightens as they talk, think and drink.

Kiwi Icons

Certain objects of everyday living are so dear to the Kiwi heart that the sight or even mention of them can bring on an instant attack of homesickness in the Kiwi abroad.

When the postal authorities chose to bring out an issue of stamps to celebrate Kiwi culture, it was not too hard to decide on ten significant items. Fish and chips, pavlova, and kiwifruit were natural contenders. The fourth raised smiles of recognition round the country and overseas – a mountainous cone of mouth-watering hokey pokey ice-cream, studded with glistening jewel-like chips of golden hokey pokey toffee which every Kiwi knows and loves.

Two items of working gear, plus one for sports and one for leisure, made up the clothing section of the stamp issue. One was the boldly checked, heavy cotton bush shirt or swanndri which is standard farm, forest and hunting wear even worn by shearers except in summer when it is swapped for a black singlet. Gumboots (never called Wellingtons) completed the working outfit. Rugby boots stood for sports in general. Leisure was summed up by what Kiwis call 'jandals'*, the thick-soled, strap-between-the-toes, beach footwear that others call thongs or flip-flops.

Paua shell or abalone was an obvious choice. Most homes have paua shell items of some kind. When not used as ash trays or soap dishes, their gleaming, pearly, iridescent insides make exquisite jewellery, or souvenir-type trinkets, such as little shell animals with paua eyes.

Highly popular was the stamp which showed a Buzzy Bee, the Kiwi designed pull-along toy for toddlers, with a scarlet body and wings and brilliant yellow and black face topped by antennae. When tugged, the contraption makes a very satisfactory noise. Most Kiwi kids can look back on a childhood enlivened by a Buzzy Bee.

* Said to come from 'Japanese sandal', since these strips of colourful rubber bear some resemblance to traditional Japanese footwear.

Culture

New Zealand's national song is *God Defend New Zealand*, to which many people add, sotto voce, "Because nobody else will".

Art critics have long accused Kiwis of the 'cultural cringe', of bowing down before anything British in preference to what comes out of New Zealand. For generations, all eyes and ears were turned to Britain – what was British was better or safer went the theory, and anything foreign was a bit threatening. Of course, anything American in this context did not count as foreign.

Television

New Zealand's primary source of culture is television. This means English, American and Aussie drama series, entertainments and documentaries, with a handful of home-grown entries. It also means innumerable imported game shows, sports and more sports, news and backgrounders – all abruptly interrupted by commercials.

A government-funded Māori TV channel has now been established to reinforce Māori culture and language. Early attempts to get the station off the ground proved highly entertaining in their own right. One set-back involved a director of the fledgling station who used government money for private purchases, including a pair of extravagantly priced boxer shorts – a public scandal which came to be known as 'UndieGate'.

TV soaps prepare the young for life as they do in most western countries. One of New Zealand's three main TV channels has a highly popular local soap, *Shortland Street*. It is set in an Auckland inner-city clinic where love affairs, misgivings, mix-ups, unwanted pregnancies, misconceptions and occasional illness and accident are swiftly dealt with for 30 minutes (less the commercial breaks) in prime time every week night. *Shortland Street* is now the main source of sex and family life education for the nation's teenagers. Not ony has the show done its bit to shape New Zealand's multi-cultural identity, it shows that Māori, Polynesian and *Pakeha* are equally adept at seduction and being misunderstood.

Literature

The unofficial poet laureate, Allen Curnow, has had his poem *Landfall in Unknown Seas* set to music by the country's leading composer, Douglas Lilburn, and read by Sir Edmund Hillary. Its first lines:

> Simply by sailing in a new direction
> You could enlarge the world.

open up the amazing possibilities of a new country. It is this newness that is always in the back of Kiwis' minds. It's part of the verve, the 'give anything a go' mind set, which is threaded through the national psyche.

Two poets, Sam Hunt and Gary McCormick, who have barnstormed the country and taken their poetry to the pubs, are equally at home out in the sticks. McCormick founded what may be the country's most popular political movement. For years, in short weekly sessions on national radio, his Pull Yourself Together Party gave bracing rallying calls and instant solutions to the woes of the week.

Other authentic Kiwi voices have not had to be so highbrow. Deer culling in the most remote reaches of the New Zealand bush produced book after book of the tallest tales by Barry Crump. The titles of his best-known are pure Kiwi in both style and substance. *A Good Keen Man* and *Hang On a Minute, Mate* are long, meandering, outback yarns which make people grin, even if they are sitting snug in their Lay-Z-Boy recliners.

It has been said of two of the most influential writers, Katherine Mansfield and Frank Sargeson, that they have afflicted New Zealand writing because many would-be authors have tried, and failed, to imitate their very different styles. However, the country's heroes remain its sports people, not its artists: not the Booker prize winner Keri Hulme with the sudden fame of her novel *The Bone People,* nor even someone as popular as detective story writer Ngaio Marsh. While Team New Zealand was celebrated with ticker tape parades both times it brought home the America's Cup, the best a successful Kiwi author can hope for is an invitation to join the Governor-General in a cup of tea.

Film

A number of Kiwi feature films have scooped awards on the international circuit. Three in particular, *The Piano,* *Once Were Warriors,* and *Heavenly Creatures,* as different from one another as they could be, demonstrated the Kiwi artist's penchant for the serious, if not downright depressing.

By contrast *Whale Rider,* the creation of writer Witi Ihimaera and director Niki Caro, tells the uplifting story of a young Māori girl's struggle to decide her future. It took everyone by surprise when it became a runaway success overseas.

But by far the biggest and most ambitious piece of Kiwi movie-making is Peter Jackson's production of Tolkien's classic, *The Lord of the Rings.* The dramatic New Zealand landscape seems to be just what Tolkien had in mind. It is now something of a Mecca for legions of Tolkien fans keen to retrace Frodo's steps towards 'Mount Doom'.

New Zealand has long been a destination of choice for international film makers in search of lush natural backdrops and relatively cheap labour. The prolific Indian film industry has been particularly taken by the scenery, and close to 100 'Bollywood' movies have been produced in whole or in part in New Zealand, including *Koi Mil Gaya* (Someone Found), India's first science-fiction musical.

Music

The Māori opera singer, Kiri Te Kanawa, is the country's darling. On her occasional visits home, thousands who would never go to an opera throng her open-air concerts.

When Māori perform at concerts, their distinctive songs (waiata) and harmonies now reflect influenes from around the world, and their musical instrument of choice is the imported guitar. Pre-European Māori music does not appeal to the modern ear – nor, indeed, to the modern Māori.

Systems

The Kiwis like to say of adversity that it's 'character forming'. This is fortunate given the many social and economic changes they've endured in one generation. In the mid-1980s, New Zealand's highly regulated economy was suddenly flung open. Government support, in the form of tariffs and subsidies for many industries, evaporated almost overnight, a large number of state-owned assets were sold to private interests, and welfare started to be scaled back. The tinkering continues, so that week to week it can be hard to work out who is running the nation's power grid, or just what style of hospital management is in vogue. Despite the upheaval, everything still works pretty well, and nobody makes too much of a fuss. Besides, the cutbacks provide limitless opportunities for having a good grumble.

Transport

Whether you go by plane, train, coach or the ferries which link the North and South Islands, long-distance public transport is generally reliable and reasonably priced. Not so public transport within cities. Bus services have been so reduced in numbers and routes that you are unlikely to get anywhere near where you want to go or when you want to go there.

Christchurch, dead flat except for its guardian Cashmere Hills, is the city of bicycles. Wellington, its harbour rimmed by hills, has cable cars and more than a quarter of the country's mountain bikes. Auckland has the worst transport problems. Its harbour bridge was not able to cope with all the traffic and an entire extra section, prefabricated in Japan, had to be attached to the side to provide more vehicle lanes. It is known as the Nippon Clip-on.

Most people own a car, sometimes two or three to a family. Kiwis love cars, no matter how old. Young people can get a probationary driving licence when they are 15. This is considered too young for today's traffic conditions, but it dates from the time when people began their working lives at the age of 14 or 15. High school grounds look like used car lots.

Road safety officers groom schoolchildren in the proper procedures so that instead of lollipop men and women shepherding the young over road crossings, Kiwi children do it themselves. It is a great honour for 10-year-olds and older to take their turn in charge of zebra crossings (with a teacher to supervise). Adults, remembering these road safety drills from their own schooldays, are careful to co-operate. Accident statistics underline the need for basic safety regulations. New Zealand's scenery is so breathtaking, and many of the roads traverse such rugged landscape that, when you are overcome by the beauties of nature, the rule is to pull well off the road and stop. Cries of wonder at mountain, wilderness and water have led to catastrophe when eyes have strayed from the road.

As the road toll continues to rise and the number of roadside crosses goes on increasing, Kiwis consider it a Fair Go for the police to erect warning notices in areas where speed cameras are operating. Motorists duly slow down, then speed up again, only to be caught just when they reckon they have left the danger zone behind.

Education

Both primary and secondary systems have four terms a year with individual schools deciding on their term dates. For families with children at different schools, the school holidays can be a nightmare of trying to merge conflicting schedules for time-honoured trips away.

School buses transport pupils back and forth, and a Correspondence School teaches the truly isolated.

Before children are born there is provision for their parents to be educated in aspects of childbirth and child rearing. This is done mainly through hospitals and a network of parents' centres which also offer support during the pre-school stage. Plunket rooms are a feature of every town. The Plunket Society (named after Lord Plunket, a Governor-General and its first patron) has a national system of nurses and voluntary committees dedicated to advising on the feeding and general care of babies and toddlers. Play centres, kindergartens and the successful *kohanga reo* (literally 'language nests') for Māori and Pacific Island children, are widely accepted as essential preparation for school itself.

Ongoing stratagems, such as work experience, attempt to keep all children busy at school, and to some extent the compulsory learning of Māori language and culture has succeeded, and not just with Māori youngsters. Many non-Māori elect to study these subjects longer than the required minimum. Young people who leave school with no qualifications face a shrinking employment pool.

A new system called Tomorrow's Schools was designed ostensibly to give parents more say in their children's education. Cunningly, it also reduces government costs, since parents have to take over much of the administration and fundraising. At school fairs it is often said, "Bet they didn't use cake stalls to fund the navy." Schools in wine-making areas tap into parents' wine-making skills. As a fund raiser, it beats making cakes.

Selling Education

Education has become a booming earner of foreign currency, bringing in even more than wine. Many thousands of foreign students come each year to enrol in secondary and tertiary institutions. Their fees enable many of the newer polytechnics, in particular, to maintain a wider range of courses, while their living expenses boost the economy.

Students come mostly from Asia, including an increasing contingent from China, and mainly they want to learn English or business studies in one form or another. Asian students are often from families who make big sacrifices to support them. They can't afford to fail and so the social side of their lives suffers. One young Thai woman said the person she knew best at university was the janitor. He was the only one around when she was in the computer lab at 3 a.m. This ferocious focus on studying leaves many Kiwi students behind.

Another big group known as 'study abroad students' comes from Europe and North America. They look on New Zealand as an exotic but safe place to study for one or two semesters. Kiwis do their best to make sure that the country lives up to this reputation.

Business

Most Kiwi businesses are small. Everyone is on first-name terms and formality is minimal. From the boss down, everybody is expected to pull their weight.

Kiwi enterprises thrive by the simple expedient of having upgraded the old pioneers' implements. Business people load themselves with cell phones, fax machines, laptops and modems, artifacts of the digital age that are the direct descendants of the piece of number eight fencing wire – i.e., the best available tool for the job.

Entrepreneurship

The relish for Giving It a Go means that Kiwis are experienced innovators. One in seven of the adult population are entrepreneurs according to a global study in which New Zealand tops the lists year after year. Bright ideas range from the vertical shaft impact rock crusher, to a process of inducting energy without the aid of wires which has led to the world's first illuminated beer tap handle. Some give rise to strange enthusiasms, such as the 'luge' – on which folk can trundle (or hurtle) under their own control down a curving concrete track – and the boysenberry ripple ice-cream, which is enjoyed by addicts as far away as Russia.

Some unique Kiwi products result from their wool, such as odour-free socks made from a non-spun version, and a fashion fabric made from a blend of merino wool and possum hair. Possum skin gloves are another way Kiwis make use of their ecological pest. Top golfers say they last ten times as long as traditional gloves. Yachties agree, adding that they don't become salt-encrusted and stiff when dry. Many people now believe it's time that conservationists came out in favour of fur coats – provided the fur comes from possums.

Kiwis.com

The Information Technology revolution is tailor-made for Kiwis. Being isolated on the world map used to mean all manner of disadvantages in competing on the world scene. Now one click of the mouse and Kiwis are bang in the centre of the action. The novelty of this has spurred unprecedented numbers to jump on the IT wagon.

Web sites both corporate and personal bloom like the flowers in spring. E-commerce flourishes. Kiwis not only flock to use it, they also make some of the tools that IT needs. The machine tools that create 70% of the computer chips used in Silicon Valley and Asia are made in Auckland.

Another Auckland company has developed Infoshare, a simple, cheap means of helping people collaborate better over the Internet, software which can assign, track and monitor what work is being done, and by whom, anywhere in the world. And Wayne Gould, a Kiwi who became a judge in Hong Kong, was the first person to develop a computer program that could mass-produce the Sudoku number puzzle. His innovation sparked the craze for this addictive brainteaser and he could now claim the New Zealand record (if they had one) for causing the most divorces of anyone on Earth.

Nasa's Jet Propulsion Unit in California has turned to New Zealand's Marshall Software to supply a version of its Internet content security software. This will help Nasa keep track of new satellites if they go missing as they have a distressing tendency to do. Kiwi physicist Sir William Pickering would have approved. He was working for the same Nasa unit in the middle of the 20th century when he produced a rocket which put satellites into space.

Exports

E-commerce provides an opportunity for the enterprising to export a wide range of innovative goods in single units (through focusing on niche marketing rather than going for volume), anything from a kitchen sink to an anchor, in this case, an anchor that can be screwed into the seabed from the surface without a diver having to descend to dangerous depths to secure it.

Kiwis are used to exporting. They discovered long ago that it was all very well making things in factories and growing produce on farms, but there have never been enough people on the domestic front to buy it all, so they have had to look for markets overseas. The staple exports of dairy produce, meat and wool, and more recently wine which gets a celebrity press in many parts of the world, are now joined by a huge variety of goods from shark cartilage, plastic playground structures and bulk aluminium, to beechwood baby cots and green-lipped mussels.

In a free market there can be some odd goings-on. The Kiwi skipper of a trans-Tasman freighter, asked what his main cargo was, replied deadpan, "We take our cheese-cake over to Oz, and we bring their cheesecake back."

The exporters' main aim, after getting the world to know just where New Zealand is, is to get the message over that it is the home of high-quality products. A campaign called 'The New Zealand Way' has the specific task of spreading the word. Basic to its message is the idea that here is a youthful country with a fresh, experimental approach. If you don't have generations of experience, you might as well try to capitalise on the fact. It was one of their own, Lord Rutherford, the first person to split the atom, who pointed out that if you come from a small country without much money, then you have to think.

The New Zealand Way logo is 'Brand New Zealand', a silver fern placed diagonally across a clean, green New Zealand, set in an ocean of blue. Kiwis who provide goods and services which meet its standards are entitled to use the marketing forces mustered behind this image.

One of the many inventive manufacturers who fit neatly into this whole concept lives on a bay in the Queen

Charlotte Sound. Each day he and his partner-wife cross the Sound to their small factory on the mainland. There they produce to their own design Naiad inflatable boats which are bought by coastguard and sea sports officials all over the world. Meantime, Christchurch-based inventor Russell Kelly has devised a pedal-powered water cleaning and filtration system that can purify 6 to 8 litres of water a minute. His cost-effective machine, which incorporates NASA-designed filtration components, is being exported to the world's poorest regions, affording clean water to regions without electricity.

Tourism

'Sustainable tourism' has gained in currency as a Kiwi catch phrase. With over a million people now making the trek each year to New Zealand's shores, there is concern that visitors will not be able to see the clean green track through the bush because of the sheer number of others trying to see it too.

There are more campsites in New Zealand than in the U.K. and France put together, and they feature apartments and cabins up to motel standard. Unlike Britain where you can never find one, public toilets exist in the tiniest of places, even 'long drop' loos in the back of beyond. Fortunately, empty space is what the Kiwi still has lots of. In a land mass only a little bigger than the United Kingdom and a little smaller than Japan, mountains, lakes, rivers, bush reserves and geo-thermal areas trip over one another. Those who appreciate a quiet hike through some pristine wilderness are spoiled for choice. About one-third of the country is designated as national park or conservation reserve where the number one rule is 'Leave only your footprints'.

New Zealand's volatile landscape makes for unexpected attractions. Its major ski-field is a live volcano which for three consecutive ski seasons had to be closed because it was spewing out great heaps of ash. On another, you ascend in a lift, take your clothes off, soak in steaming hot springs, put your clothes back on, and ski down again.

For most people few things beat a boat trip along one of the many rivers, riding the rapids or 'jet sprinting' which provides the thrill of propulsion at near supersonic speeds with vertigo-inducing G-force on the turns. It's all part of the pioneering experience. The latest leisure development caters to nature of a different sort. To counter criticism that all there is on offer is the scenery, grandiose casinos have been established. Kiwis appear to be the main patrons. Visitors are too busy looking at the view.

Health and Welfare

The Kiwis see themselves as a nation of hunters and mountain climbers and general risk-takers, and every weekend there are enough accidents and search-and-rescue parties underway to prove it.

Taking too much care of oneself goes against the pioneering spirit. Males in particular see it as bad form to whine about being under the weather. On the farm, in the bush, or on the rugby field, any condition less severe than a coma is to be 'played through'. Any bloke who snivels to his mates that he's feeling "a bit crook" and had better spend the day in bed is likely to be threatened with being put on the first plane to Sydney.

However, when Kiwis really 'take sick' they expect to be looked after. Whatever their condition, they expect not just health services, but also the provision of housing, welfare and superannuation. This expectation dates from the days when the country considered itself the social welfare laboratory of the world. In the current climate of reduced staff and hospital wards, Kiwis do their best not to develop conditions requiring non-urgent surgery. Unless they have private health insurance, they face long waiting lists.

Cost cutting has also reduced the Accident Compensation Commission to a shadow of its original self. A bold undertaking when first established, it entitled anyone who was accidentally injured to compensation and rehabilitation – even the burglar who, in attempting to break a window, cut his hand.

These days everyone has to pay when consulting a doctor unless they have a special concession. The new emphasis on individual responsibility for keeping well and thus saving the state money has led to a rash of Wellness Clinics, and this is the one aspect of the (otherwise disliked) health reforms which meets with general approval. People plan to live long, and most of them do.

With all that sunshine, good butter, cream and fat lamb in their youth, heart disease and other effects of high cholesterol intake, plus cancer, especially melanoma, are the most feared and talked-about illnesses. Being overweight is commonplace and weight-loss courses are big business. 'UV' (ultra violet light) is now an established term in everyday language. It is an Aussie canard that Kiwi sheep have to wear sunglasses, but most people wear sun hats and sunscreen, and the bronzed hunks of yesteryear are looked at askance. They are either mad, or visiting Californians.

New Zealand used to be a nation of premature denture-wearers, though more because many water supplies lacked essential minerals than through neglect. The free and very necessary dental service for all schoolchildren was a source of national pride. Dentists were the highest earners of all professionals. Since the fluoridation of most of the water supplies, however, dental health has improved to a point where dentists, it is said, have had to sell their second yachts.

Crime and Punishment

Kiwi cops do not carry guns unless on special alert. If on occasion there is an accusation of police brutality or over-zealousness, uproar continues until the matter is sorted out. Kiwis like their police to be above reproach.

Most people are reasonably law-abiding. Corruption is rare, so it is big news when people in high places are caught tax-dodging or something even more heinous. Perpetrators of white-collar crime and corporations suspected of being 'on the take', or at least sailing close to the wind, are despised and resented. They are commonly believed to be putting themselves beyond the ken of everyday detective work by means of computer fraud or complex transactions off-shore which gives them an unfair advantage over the ordinary bloke giving crime a go – it's just not playing the game.

Thefts and burglaries top the list of petty crimes, except perhaps in the far north of the country, where a good living can be made tending a marijuana crop. Known as New Zealand Green or 'electric *puha*' (its pseudo Māori name), it is illegal despite a widespread push toward decriminalisation. Police use helicopters to try to suss out thriving plantations – tricky when it comes to the new hydroponic crops, grown indoors.

Nor are they helped by the public attitude. A respected pensioner wanted to repair the cracked driveway of the state house he rented. The authorities refused to cough up for new concrete. He worked out how many marijuana plants he would need to grow and sell to pay for his spot of DIY. The gardening went well. Then he was discovered, and his simple plan aired in court. The country was shocked. This was not a Fair Go. Donations to the pensioner streamed in, more than enough for the most impressive landscaping. It's an attitude that is also reflected in a growing political movement to decriminalize marijuana possession. From the 'grassroots', so to speak.

Kiwi prisons are referred to as 'colleges of crime' and a raft of alternative punishments and rehabilitation measures are attempted in the country's jails to keep malefactors from becoming better 'educated'. Most appear to fail, so the recidivism rate remains high. Some prisons, such as Auckland's forbidding Mount Eden, might have come straight from the pages of Dickens. On the other hand, those to which non-violent first offenders are sent are called 'country clubs'.

Two initiatives have been copied by other nations. The first is a passionately led movement for restorative justice. Here the offender and the victim are brought together in a controlled situation with the dual aim of trying to make amends to the victim in some way as well as getting the perpetrator to face up to wrong-doing.

The second is victim support, where teams automatically swing into action after serious crimes, including burglary. One such support team arrived to counsel a householder after the theft of his lawnmower. He would survive the trauma, he assured them. He and his lawnmower were "only on nodding terms".

Government

At first glance the mechanisms of Kiwi government look simple. There is one Parliament with no Upper House. A Governor-General represents the British Crown, and though the notion of moving towards a republic has growing support, the country is an ardent and loyal member of the British Commonwealth.

In the country's private sector, men still far out-number women in positions of power and influence and in earning capacity. In government, however, women rule: at one point, the Governor-General, prime minister, leader of the opposition, attorney-general, and chief justice were all female. Women explain this by saying that cream rises to the top.

There is one set of laws for the whole country – none of your Aussie-type separate states' legislation here. Voting, on the other hand, has become a little more complicated since the introduction of MMP (Mixed Member Proportional) representation. Previously a national election was run under a straight one-vote system, the winner being the first past the post. With MMP, each citizen now has two votes: one for the electoral candidate, the other (known as the list vote) for one of the registered political parties. The more list votes a party gets, the more parliamentary seats it is entitled to.

Kiwis opted for MMP in the hope of everyone being represented, minority viewpoints getting a fair hearing, a reduction of the gap between the haves and have-nots, and a guarantee of a 'culture of consensus'. In the first years of MMP coalition government it became evident that these fine ideals could be undermined since a minority party is able to hold a majority party to ransom if that party is so keen to build alliances it makes big concessions to a small potential ally. What is more, the large number of small parties all wanting to Give It a Go can mean that none wins an electorate seat, or secures the minimum 5% of list votes otherwise needed to qualify for a seat in parliament.

All these possibilities make Kiwis a little uneasy. Nevertheless, the MMP system is all about the good results that can emerge from a little bit of squabbling. In any case, with so many good women running the show, nothing can go too wrong. This, like so many other of New Zealand's great experiments, is still on trial. Whatever the outcome Kiwis are resigned to hopes being raised, then dashed again. Achieving a Fair Go was never easy.

Language and Accent

Strange greetings bemuse the visitor to New Zealand. All are expected to learn the friendly Māori greeting '*kia ora*' which is used liberally by Māori and *Pakeha* alike. Once you get to know a Kiwi, expect a 'chur bro' or 'howzit goin' on arriving, and a surprising 'hooray' as you leave.

The language is littered with oddities. In public bars in the north of the country there is apt to be a notice saying 'No patches'. This has nothing to do with pirates. Patches are gang regalia and are prohibited as being likely to provoke a fight. Farther south a billboard might proclaim, 'Old Man's Beard Must Go'. It is not meant to discriminate. Old Man's Beard is an imported variety of clematis which thrives so well in New Zealand that it threatens to strangle native plants.

Spoken sentences often end on a rising inflection, especially if they have the matey 'eh' tacked on to them. "We're going to the pictures, eh" – their ingrained politeness leaving the ending open so as to give the recipient a chance to respond.

Sex is an uncomfortable topic of conversation for the polite Kiwi. To avoid having to say the 's' word, an amorous Kiwi bloke might only confess to "being a bit randy" or to wanting to "let the ferret out for a run". Be wary, though. Even these polite phrases, said in the wrong company, might result in a 'knuckle sandwich' (i.e. a punch in the 'laughing gear').

Visitors need to listen carefully to how Kiwis pronounce their words. Vowel sounds can be a trap. The story is told of the Kiwi hostess who telephoned to invite an American businessman to bring his wife to stay in her unfinished home, still uncarpeted, and with bare concrete floors. "I warn you," she said, "it's pretty basic. There may be sacks on the floor." There was a slight pause, then the gallant American came back with an accommodating, "Sex on the floor, sex anywhere."

The Authors

A fifth-generation New Zealander, Christine Cole Catley has forebears from England and Scotland and a Swedish great-grandfather. Most of them were sheep farmers and she grew up on a North Island sheep farm not far from the small town named after another of her great-grandfathers, James Bull. It is 'the only place where you can get milk from Bulls'.

She went to university in the South Island, spent most of her working life in Wellington as a journalist, advertising copywriter (it was she who came up with the name kiwiberry), television critic, broadcaster and teacher of journalism, then went south again.

Now based in Auckland she writes, reads, works as a book publisher, runs writers' workshops, gardens, and goes out on the water whenever she can – that is, when she isn't travelling. Her three children all live overseas, and she is on her fifth passport.

Simon Nicholson grew up in Rotorua, a central North Island town. He spent a good deal of his early life providing instruction on the art of riding Rotorua's famous 'luge'. He also became expert at constructing ad hoc travel itineraries for tourists eager to see as much of New Zealand as possible inside 10 days.

Presently on his O.E. completing doctoral work in Washington, D.C., he spends his free time fielding questions about *The Lord of the Rings*, and searching for bars that screen rugby matches. Despite numerous attempts, he has yet to make a pavlova that's worth eating.
